REVOLUTION IN THE SUNNAH

Ghazi A. Algosaibi

REVOLUTION IN THE SUNNAH

Translated from the Arabic by
Leslie McLoughlin

SAQI

British Library Cataloguing-in-Publication Data
A catalogue for this book is available from the
British Library

ISBN 0 86356 345 7
EAN 9 780863 56345 4

This edition first published 2004

Saqi Books
26 Westbourne Grove
London W2 5RH
www.saqibooks.com

Contents

A Note on Sources

All *Hadiths* in this little book are quoted from the collections of authentic *Hadiths* approved by a consensus of scholars, in line with the basic principles set out by *Hadith* scholars in the established sources.

The reference upon which I have largely relied is the encyclopaedic book titled *Jami' al-Usul fi Ahadith al-Rasul*, by the Imam Abi al-Sa'adat Mubarak bin Muhammad ibn al-Athir al-Jazari. The specific edition used was edited by Muhammad al-Fiqi, published under the supervision of Sheikh Abdul Majid Salim by the Department for Scientific Research, Fatwa, Da'wa and Guidance, Kingdom of Saudi Arabia (first edition, 1370 AH/1950 AD).

Introduction

*In the name of Allah, the Most Merciful,
the Most Compassionate*

Some people may think it is risky to give a collection of seven short essays such a sensational title. I would beg to differ. A revolution involves a radical and comprehensive change in the status quo. The *Hadiths* I will discuss in these essays were a real 'revolution' that radically changed the backward, pre-Islamic conditions of life in a number of crucial areas. I would even go so far as to say that they continue to represent a real 'revolution' against the outmoded and discredited practices prevailing in these areas of life in some, if not the vast majority, of Muslim countries.

This rapid survey of the treasures of the Traditions of the Prophet (peace be upon him) is simply an invitation to other researchers to undertake wider and deeper expeditions to achieve our hoped-for objective: that Muslims who seek reform understand in their hearts that Islam contains the guidance they require. They do not need to import reform from abroad, provided the opportunistic selectivity with which Islam is practised in Muslim countries is brought to an end.

ONE

Integrity in Political Life

Text of the *Hadith*

The Messenger of Allah (pbuh) apppointed a man from the Azd tribe called Ibn Lutbiyya to be in charge of *Sadaqa*. This meant authorising him to receive gifts of alms from the people on behalf of the State. The man duly came back to the Prophet, saying, 'This wealth is for you [i.e. for the public treasury] and this is a gift presented to me.'

The Prophet got up, praised God and extolled Him, then said:

'I appoint a man from among you, sharing in the authority that Allah has entrusted to me, and he comes to me saying: "This wealth is for you and this is a gift presented to me!" Why did he not remain in the house of his father and his mother until his gift came to him, if he were truthful? By Allah, any one of you who takes anything to which he is not entitled shall meet his Lord carrying it on himself on the Day of Judgement. I will disown any one of you [on that day] who meets Allah while carrying a screaming camel, a bellowing cow or a bleating goat.'

Then he raised his hands so high that the whiteness of his armpits could be seen and said: 'O my Lord, have I truly conveyed Thy Commandments?'

Narrated on the authority of Abi Hamid al-Sa'idi, reported by al-Bukhari, Muslim and Abu Dawud.

(*Jami' al-Usul*, Part V, pp. 355–6.)

Commentary

In most if not all Muslim countries, many factors coalesce to make corruption a widespread phenomenon that undermines the very foundations of society. Among those factors, we can mention the following just for the sake of illustration, not in order to be exhaustive:

> There is the fact that small elites monopolise resources at the expense of the majority;
> there is an absence of institutions protecting public money;
> there is a weakness of moral imperatives.

These, along with other negative factors, stem at the end of the day from one core reason, which is the lack of freedom, whether we call it compulsory consultation [*Shura*] or democracy or pluralism. Alas, the issue of freedom will have to be left for another long discussion – a very long one, in fact.

The spread of corruption among Muslims had led to the emergence of a malevolent idea in the West which argues that there is some kind of relationship between Islam, as a religion and set of laws, and corruption as a social phenomenon. It should suffice, in this context, to give just one example of the pervasiveness of this concept that the word *bakshish* has come to be synonymous in Western perception with all forms of corruption. The point here is not whether the word's origins are Arab,

Turkish or Persian but that, in the West, it is considered a word of Muslim origin.

No one disputes the fact that a number of Muslims, be it small or large, are corrupt. The real question is: Does this corruption have anything to do with the religion to which they belong, or is it in clear contravention of its tenets? The above *Hadith* should suffice to show that Islam fought against corruption and its perpetrators, promising them so terrible a punishment on the Day of Judgement that hearts would quake at the thought.

When was the Prophet talking about the terrible fate awaiting the corrupt? He spoke at a time when Muslims had only recently emerged from an age of darkness and ignorance whose slogan was: 'To the victor, the spoils'. He spoke to a small, nascent society that knew nothing of civil service, addressed a people for whom hunger was the norm.

I wish that every Muslim country would place this *Hadith* on the cover of the code of conduct it issues to its officials and employees; that every management school would teach it to its students; that it would hang on the walls of every government office.

The Prophet described the punishment that will befall those who meet God on the Day of Judgement carrying a bribe in the form of a camel. How much worse off will we in the employ of government be if we stand before God on the Day of Judgement carrying our ill-gotten gains in the form of a fleet of luxury cars or a block of flats twenty stories high?

The most terrible chastisement will be the reward of the man who turns up on the Day of Judgement carrying an entire country he purloined in the middle of the night through a military coup.

TWO

Women's Role in Society (and in the Military!)

Text of the *Hadith*

Whenever the Messenger of Allah (pbuh) went to Quba', he used to visit Um Haram bint Milhan, who would feed him. She was the wife of 'Ubada bin al-Samit. One day, the Prophet went to her house and she gave him a meal … He fell asleep. He woke up laughing.

She asked him: 'What makes you laugh, O Messenger of Allah?'

He said: 'Some people of my followers were displayed before me as warriors fighting for the Cause of Allah and sailing over this sea, kings on thrones.'

She said: 'O Messenger of Allah! Invoke Allah that He may make me one of them.' He invoked (Allah) for her and then laid down his head and slept again. Then once again he woke up laughing.

She asked: 'What makes you laugh, O Messenger of Allah?'

He said: 'Some people of my followers were displayed before me as warriors fighting for the Cause of Allah', and he repeated what he had said the first time.

She said: 'O Messenger of Allah! Invoke Allah that He may make me one of them.'

He said: 'You will be amongst the first ones.'

Um Haram sailed out to sea during the reign of Mu'awiyah bin Abi Sufyan, and upon disembarking she fell off her riding animal and died.

Narrated on the authority of Anas bin Malik, reported by al-Bukhari, Muslim, Malik, al-Tirmidhi, Abu Dawud and al-Nisa'i.

(*Jami' al-Usul*, Part X, pp. 95–8.)

Commentary

The real disagreement between Muslims, jurists and lay-men alike, regarding women is not between those who think a woman's clothes may allow her face and the palms of her hands to show and those who maintain that a woman's clothing should show nothing of her whatsoever. If the disagreement were concerned with such minutiae, matters would be much easier, regardless of which camp one decided to follow, especially as the reference books of Islamic jurisprudence provide ample support for either position.

The principal dispute, the real nature of which is never spelled out, is between two distinct camps. On one side are those who believe that women are the partners and sisters of men; that, exactly like men, they have rights and responsibilities; that the custodianship of men over women should be seen as a trust for which men are responsible, not a means for the denigration of women. On the opposing side are those who believe that women are lesser creatures; that their one and only role is childbearing; that their movement should be restricted to transfer from their fathers' homes to their husbands', and from the latter's to the grave; that 'the burial of girls is a blessed act!'. Indeed, our heritage bequeathed a famous, much quoted verse of poetry ot the effect that women have no rights, except to make men 'sexually satisfied'.

Those who hold the first opinion also think that women have the right to the highest possible levels of education; to be creative and productive in all areas of intellectual and scientific endeavour; to become active participants in the political life of society. Those who adhere to the second opinion prefer to deprive women of any type of knowledge or intellectual life. They seek to stifle all the potential, capability and talent Allah endowed women with, and to confine them to one sole role in life, a role that begins and ends with sex.

Unlike what most people imagine, the debate between the two camps does not take place in the refined courts of jurisprudence. It is a psychological, political, social and cultural struggle between men who believe that the recognition of women's rights enriches their own lives, and men who believe that such recognition negates their masculinity. This kind of dispute can only continue indefinitely. No amount of debate and discussion could bring it to a conclusion.

The *Hadith* which I have quoted here shows with incomparable clarity how the Prophet, the Imam who leads us to True Guidance, sees woman's role in society (and in the military!): he believed it should include going out to sea on military expeditions in the company of men. Of the followers of our Imam I am one, regardless of what some may say.

THREE

The Rules of Proof Safeguard Rights

Text of the *Hadith*

Abu Huraira reported that Sa'ad bin Ubada said: 'O Messenger of Allah, if I were to find a man alone with my wife, should I wait until I bring four witnesses?'

The Prophet (pbuh) said: 'Yes.' (*Hadith* confirmed by Muslim and al-Muwatta'.)

According to the version of Muslim and Abu Dawud, Abu Huraira reported that Sa'ad bin Ubada said: 'O Messenger of Allah, do you think that a man, if he were to find another man with his wife, is entitled to kill him?'

The Messenger of Allah said: 'No.'

'By God, that cannot be so', said Sa'ad.

The Messenger of Allah replied [in amazement]: 'Listen to what Sa'ad has said!'

(*Jami' al-Usul*, Part IV, p. 265.)

Commentary

This wonderful insistence that a person is innocent until proven guilty, and that guilt may only be proven through specific, established procedures, did not come down to us as part of the heritage of Roman law; nor was it produced in Europe during the Renaissance. It did not arrive with the liberal ideas that invaded the world during the past two centuries; nor was it the product of the Marxist interpretation of history, based on dialectical materialism.

This insistence on 'innocent until proven guilty' was pronounced by the Prophet fourteen centuries ago, in a tribal, unenlightened society that had not even heard of the rules of evidence and proof, at least in connection with women committing adultery. In that society, killing a woman on grounds of suspicion alone was acceptable, indeed desirable, in order to protect the purity of family honour.

The Prophet of Islam, with this pioneering directive, was not only ahead of his contemporaries and those who went before them, but he set a precedent for courts everywhere today.

Courts continue to treat crimes of honour, the so-called 'crimes of passion', in a special way, which culminates in a reduced sentence for the convicted husband. I recall a friend, a US lawyer, once telling me: 'Give me a man who killed his wife in an honour case and I will guarantee you that the jury in any US court would acquit him.'

Likewise, the statutes of a vast number of countries

around the world, including Muslim countries, incorporate articles taken from French law requiring that a cuckolded husband accused of killing his wife must be treated with unparalleled gentleness.

Alas, Muslim jurists, who have taken the greatest care in studying all aspects of Islamic law, did not pay the attention deserved to the rules governing judicial procedures, and especially to the principles of evidence and proof. Even contemporary writings on Islamic jurisprudence suffer from this oversight. The result is that fundamental rights guaranteed by clear references in the Holy Qur'an and the Sunnah have, in practice, been neglected in the implementation. Muslims benefit nothing from a right which any member of the executive authorities, or even the judiciary, can violate simply by deciding that the common weal requires that this right be ignored.

Without established – I am almost tempted to say revered – rules for judicial proceedings, there will be no firm guarantees for anyone. Without firm guarantees, fundamental rights can vanish into thin air, even if reiterated in a thousand constitutions.

The treasures of the Sunnah still wait to be extracted from the established sources of correct *Hadiths*, not to be interpreted and explained – a task already achieved by great jurists and scholars past and present – but to be turned into strict legislation which applies to rulers before it applies to the ruled, and which becomes an integral part of daily life in every Muslim society.

FOUR

The Sanctity of Private Life

The Text of the *Hadiths*

Narrated by Anas bin Malik:

'A man peeped into a room of the Prophet (pbuh), who then stood up and aimed an arrow at him. It was as if I was seeing him trying to find the man to stab him.'

(Reported by Bukhari and Muslim.)

Al-Bukhari's version states:

> 'A man peeped into the house of the Prophet and the Prophet aimed an arrow at him.'

Abu Dawud also reported the first version.

Al-Tirmidhi reported the following version:

> 'The Prophet was in his home when a man peeped in on him. The Prophet threw an arrow at him, so the man retreated.'

In An-Nisa'i's version:

> 'A Bedouin man came to the door of Prophet and placed his eye on a gap in the door. The Prophet saw him and aimed an iron rod – or a stick – at him to pierce his eye. When the man saw him he retreated. The Prophet told him: "If you had stayed put I would have pierced your eyes."'

Narrated by Sahl bin Sa'ad:

> 'A man peeped through a hole in the door of the Prophet while the Prophet was holding an iron comb with which he was combing his hair. The Prophet said: "Had I known you were looking (through the hole), I would have pierced your eye

with the comb." Verily! We were commanded to seek permission precisely so that one would not see things unlawfully.'

(Reported by al-Bukhari, Muslim, an-Nisa'i and al-Tirmidhi.)

Narrated by Abu Huraira:

'The Prophet said:

"If any person peeps into someone's house without permission, they are allowed to pierce his eye."'

In another version, Abu Huraira narrated that he heard the Prophet say:

'If anyone peeps into your house without your permission and you throw a pebble at him and pierce his eye, there will be no offence committed.'

(Reported by al-Bukhari and Muslim.)

In the version reported by Abu Dawud:

'... without their permission and they gouged his eye, he has forfeited his eye.'

In the version reported by al-Nisa'i, the Prophet said:

'Anyone who peeps into people's homes without their permission and they pierce his eye, there shall be no recompense and no punishment.'

In another version, the Prophet said:

'If someone peeps in on you without permission and you throw [something] at him and pierce his eye, you won't be blamed.'

Or, according to another version:

'… you will have committed no wrong.'

(*Jami' al-Usul*, Part VII, pp. 376–78.)

Commentary

It is curious – and I do not know whether we should laugh or cry – that we Muslims have left these *Hadiths* in their reference sources, being content just to read them without deriving the legislation that guarantees the protection of people's private lives. Stranger still, the non-Muslim West surrounds people's private lives with formidable laws which guarantee them protection. In the West, to which we never tire of ascribing every shortcoming, if a police-man enters the home of a citizen (or even of an alien!) without going through the onerous procedures laid down in law, his infringement will be pronounced illegal, thus nullifying all successive steps he takes, leading to the defendant being acquitted in court even if he is (plainly) guilty.

Also in the West, eavesdropping on telephone conver-sations or intercepting postal correspondence is a criminal offence under the law. The state may only resort to such methods when absolutely necessary, and even then only with the permission of a specific competent authority. In the West, every person has the right to go to court to pro-tect his private life against any invasion, whatever its nature or source.

On the other hand, in all parts of our Muslim world without exception, people, be they friend or foe, barge into one's home unannounced and uninvited. This is what ordinary people do. The authorities, however behave as though they own people's homes. They enter whenever they please. They will send in their dawn raiders or visitors who arrive unannounced in broad daylight or as night falls. Tapping phone conversations has ceased to be the prerogative of specialized agencies and is now available to all, amateurs and professionals alike. The Muslim world is full of groups that break down front doors and force their way into people's homes on the pretext of preventing immorality and defending virtue. And no one censures them, let alone gouges out their eyes.

The renaissance of Islam can not be achieved by learning religious texts by heart and reciting them for public show. It can only come about by turning those texts into a vital part of every Muslim's life, in every Muslim society, each and every day. How I wish that all those movements acting under the banner of Islam would include in their program legislation that protects the sanctity of the private lives of Muslims, instead of rushing to compete in the elimination of the last remnants of privacy.

The English have a celebrated saying:

> 'An Englishman's home is his castle.'

It is Muslims above all who should have a similar saying.

FIVE

The Prevention of Cruelty to Animals

Text of the *Hadiths*

Narrated by Abu Huraira:

'The Messenger of Allah (pbuh) said: "While a man was walking he felt thirsty and went down a well and drank water from it. On coming out of it, he saw a dog panting and eating earth because of excessive thirst. The man said: 'This dog is suffering from the same thirst as I.'

"So he went down the well, filled his shoe with water, held it in his teeth and climbed up and gave water to the dog. Allah thanked him [for his good deed] and forgave him.

"The people then asked: 'O Messenger of Allah! Is there a reward for us in serving animals?'

"He replied: 'Yes, there is a reward for serving any animate creature.'"

In another account, The Messenger of Allah said:

'A prostitute saw a dog on a hot day going round and round a well, with his tongue hanging out because of thirst. She took off her shoe for him [to bring water to him]. So Allah forgave her because of that.'

In another account, the Prophet said:

'While a dog was going round and round a well and was about to die of thirst, a prostitute saw it and took off her shoe and watered the dog with it. So Allah forgave her because of that good deed.'

(Reported by al-Bukhari and Muslim.)

Al-Bukhari also narrated the following *Hadith*:

'The Prophet said: "A man saw a dog eating mud from [the severity of] thirst. So, that man took a shoe and filled it with water and kept on pouring the water for the dog until it quenched its thirst. So Allah approved of his deed and caused him to enter Paradise."'

(al-Muwatta' and Abu Dawud reported the first account.)

Narrated by Abdullah bin 'Umar:

'The Prophet said: "A woman entered Hell because of a cat which she had tied up, neither giving it food nor setting it free to eat from the insects of the earth."'

In another account:

'The Messenger of Allah said: "A woman was put in Hell because of a cat which she had kept locked up till it died. She neither fed it nor watered it when she locked it up, nor did she set it free to eat the insects of the earth."'

(Reported by al-Bukhari and Muslim.)

Narrated by Abu Huraira:

'I heard the Messenger of Allah say: "An ant had bitten a Prophet (one amongst the earlier Prophets) and he ordered that the colony of ants be burnt. Allah revealed to him: 'Because of an ant's bite you have burnt a community from amongst the communities which sings My glory?!'"

(*Jami' al-Usul*, Part V, pp. 274–8.)

Commentary

In the West, if a falcon is discovered, injured and far from its nest, it turns into a society star. The news media cover its every move and report every fresh development in its medical condition, and donations pour in from every side. When a whale loses its way amid a sea of icebergs, a state of emergency is declared and the head of state himself will take command of a national campaign to rescue it. When a major dam project threatens a species of tiny reptiles with extinction, wildlife conservationists rise as one, the dam project collapses and the small reptiles survive another day.

In Muslim countries children amuse themselves in the streets with dogs in full view of adults. They pelt them with stones, drag them by the neck and break their limbs. Only a painful death delivers the hapless dogs from their torturers. We see owners of donkeys, mules or camels weighing them down with loads that could break their backs. As for the killing of sparrows and other birds, parents and children alike compete in this popular hobby.

Before anyone jumps up to explain and correct, I recognize that the West, which is so extravagant in its desire for the protection of a single animal, cares not a jot for the hardship experienced by entire nations. I also recognize that the examples I attributed to Muslim countries do not apply to all Muslims. These facts I am totally convinced of. What concerns me in this context is that the care shown to animals by the West exceeds, many times over, the care shown by the Muslim East. I don't think anyone would argue with this specific point.

Is it not sad, and astonishing, that the *Hadiths* of the Prophet inform us that a prophet was rebuked because of an ant, that a woman was put in Hell because of a cat she had locked up, that Allah forgave a prostitute her sins because of a dog she had relieved of thirst. Yet Muslims treat God's other creatures as though they were enemies in an unequal war of mutual destruction.

Someone may ask: 'Are you asking for the establishment of Islamic organisations for animal protection when we haven't established such organisation for humans?' I have no words to respond to this.

But there is something I'd like to say: if this is the respect Islam shows for animal life, how long will we allow dissolute and oppressive individuals and regimes to abuse human life as they please, in the name of Islam?

SIX

Family Planning

The Text of the *Hadiths*

Abu Sa'id al Khadri related the following:

'We went out with The Messenger of Allah (pbuh) on the expedition to the Bani al-Mustaliq and captured some concubines [as part of the spoils]; and we desired them, for we were suffering from the absence of our wives, and we wished to have sexual intercourse with them, observing *'azl* (*coitus interruptus*, or the withdrawal of the male sexual organ before emission of semen to avoid conception). But we said: "We are doing an act before asking the Messenger of Allah who is amongst us?" So we asked The Messenger of Allah, and he said:

"It does not matter if you do not do it, for every soul that is to be born up to the Day of Resurrection will be born.'"

There is another similar account that mentions that the Prophet said:

'It does not matter if you do not do it, for every soul that Allah has destined to be born shall be born.'

Another version uses the phrase 'every soul … shall come forth.'

Another account states:

'It does not matter if you do not do it, for Allah has preordained all his creation to the Day of Judgement.'

(Reported by al-Bukhari and Muslim.)

Narrated by Jabir bin Abdullah:

'We used to practice *'azl* during the time of the

Prophet, while the Qur'an was being revealed.' This is reported by al- Bukhari and Muslim. Muslim also adds: 'We used to practice *'azl* during the time of the Prophet, and when he heard about this he did not forbid us.'

(*Jami' al-Usul*, Part XII, pp. 173–5.)

Commentary

I don't think any reasonable person would argue with the idea that when God created man and woman he also gave them the impulse to procreate, for purposes stemming from His Wisdom, perhaps primary among them being that without this impulse the human race would wither and disappear within a few generations. I don't think any reasonable person would claim that God, the Omniscient, the Wise, created us so that we should end up with such collective suicide.

Therefore, the advocacy of birth control acts against the very requirements of our nature, and contradicts the natural laws God set for man. Advocating birth control should be opposed by wise law and healthy opinion.

One of the forms of birth control is when parents restrict reproduction to a single offspring, for fear of wasting all their time on child rearing. This is the attitude of most people in the industrialised world, and of their emulators in the developing world. As a result, population growth in industrialised societies is falling so evidently that intellectuals are sounding the alarm bells, warning that continuous decline would lead to collapse.

The other side of the coin is that we see people who cannot afford to support a single child doing their best to produce the largest possible number of children, for selfish reasons related more to their own interests than those of their children – whether their aim is to show off their sexual prowess or to acquire the largest number of future, free labourers. Once the children of such parents are born, they are left without an education, healthcare or food, abandoned to disease and hunger. They are born to face a dark future. If they survive childhood diseases, they will fall prey to illnesses that afflict young people and old alike, or be met by the dismal prospect of a life of unemployment in societies that do not guarantee their citizens the minimum requirement for survival. The huge population increase in developing countries is a ticking bomb, threatening to cause inevitable and remorseless states of famine.

God's eternal laws, which protect human survival on this earth, provide that there are cases where necessity, not perceived or imagined but real and urgent, requires temporary birth control, and I emphasise the temporary nature of such birth control. As for those who claim that Islam prohibits birth control under any circumstances, as some religions do, I can only ask them to refer back with an open mind to *Hadiths* related to the issue of *'azl*.

SEVEN

The Prohibition of Torture of All Kinds

Text of the *Hadiths*

Narrated by Hisham bin Hakim bin Azzam:

'I passed by some Nabateans in Syria who had been made to stand in the sun while oil was poured upon their heads. I asked: "What is this?" It was said: "They are being tortured because

of [failure to pay] the *kharaj* [government tax]."
Thereupon I said that I had heard the Prophet of
Allah (pbuh) say:

"Allah will torment those who use torture in this
world.'"

In another account he said:

'I bear testimony to the fact that I heard The
Messenger of Allah saying: "Allah shall torment
those who torture people in this world."'

He added:

'Their ruler at the time was 'Umair bin Sa'eed,
Governor of Palestine. So I went to him and told
him about them, so they were set free.'

(Reported by Muslim.)

In the version reported by Abu Dawud:

'Hisham bin Hakim, while he was the ruler of
Hums, found a man who had been forcing some
Copts to stand in the sun in connection with the
dues of *jizya* [tax]. He said: "What is this? I heard
The Messenger of Allah saying: 'Allah shall torment
those who torment people in this world.'"'

Muslim reported in his version:

> 'I bear testimony that I heard the Prophet of Allah say that Allah will torment those who inflict torture in this world.
>
> 'As Umair bin Sa'eed was the Governor of Palestine, I went and told him what was happening and he ordered the men to be released.'

In the version related by Abu-Dawud Hisham bin Hakim when he was Governor of Hums, he found a man forcing some Copts to stand in the sun in connection with the dues of Jizya.

He said, 'What is this? I have heard the Messenger of Allah say that Allah will torment those who inflict torture in this world.'

Muslim also has a version which runs:

> 'When he was Governor of Hums he found a man exposing some Copts to the torture of the sun because of non-payment of Jizya. And then he related the *Hadith*.'

(*Jami' al-Usul*, Part XII, p. 335.)

Commentary

There is a strange, rare and terrifying book in seven volumes written by an Iraqi researcher, Abbud al-Shalgi, titled *Encyclopaedia of Torture*. It recounts in detail the myriad forms of torture meted out by Sultans and other rulers throughout Muslim history. I recommend that every educated Muslim read this book ,as it would make them realise immediately the reason why freedom and respect for human dignity still remains as far as could be from our grasp.

To give an idea of what the book contains, here are the titles of some chapters: 'Torture by Thirst'; 'Torture by Hunger'; 'Torture by Opening the Veins'; 'Killing by Breaking the Back'; 'Killing by Ripping Open the Stomach'; 'Killing by Driving Nails in the Ear'; 'Killing by Throwing to the Lions'; 'Killing by Severing the Limbs'; 'Killing and Torture by Peeling the Skin'; 'Killing by Sawing'; 'Torturing Women with Fire'; 'Torturing Women by Exposing their Genitals'. I will leave the horrifying details to the book.

From this journey into history, with its good and its evil, I return to the present to recount two events that took place in Muslim countries. The first happened to the son of a friend, the second to a relative of mine.

The friend's son was in a car driven by a colleague when they had a traffic accident. The driver was taken to the police station for investigation and my friend's son went along as a witness. While he was talking to the duty officer, this eminent functionary realised that the witness was not addressing him with the degree of respect which was owing to his high status. The officer's reaction was to accuse the witness of being ill-mannered. The latter, politely, protested against this accusation, which only angered the officer further. He summoned a constable over and whispered in his ear.

The soldier then took the witness out into the station courtyard where he beat him with thick electric wires until blood flowed from his back. Later, the poor witness appealed in vain for justice. In spite of reliable medical reports, the intercession of well-intentioned people and witness statements, the officer's superiors decided that the complaint was malicious and the file was closed. The scars remain to this very day on the back that was 'treated' with wires.

The story of my relative is less shocking. A piece of jewelry belonging to his wife had gone missing one day, and he went to the nearest police station to report it. The duty officer asked whether he employed domestic staff, to which he replied that there were two in addition to a woman cook. When the officer then asked if he accused any of them, he said that he trusted them and believed the thief came from outside the house. However, the officer assured him that the jewelry would be found as soon as he started to 'play the music'. My relative didn't understand the allusion, so the officer explained that he would sum-mon the domestics; then the cane would start to play its tunes on their bodies, until one or all of them confessed to the theft. The man was startled. He returned home and brought his wife the glad tidings that she had 'lost' the jewelry but gained the prize of sparing her employees the experience of 'music playing'.

If this is what happens in public at police stations, shouldn't we wonder what happens to political opponents in the cellars of the security organisations? We find one answer in the *Encyclopaedia of Torture*, which speaks about immersion in containers of filth, adding that this one of the forms of torture which has been practised in some Arab countries in the second half of the twentieth century.

Is it any wonder, therefore, that international conventions prohibiting torture and indicting its practitioners are drawn up by non-Muslims and are forcibly imposed on Muslims? Are we not ashamed when we see the uproar that happens in the West when one policeman is caught hitting a citizen, while beating up citizens in Muslim countries is seen as a daily routine in which policemen engage along with their other daily duties? If I had anything to do with it a subject called 'Allah Torments Those Who Torture Others on This Earth' would be made compulsory at every police academy in Muslim countries. If I had any power I would impose the teaching of this subject on anyone who has the authority to order beatings, detentions or 'immersions'.